GEORGE STEPHENSON
THE TRAIN MAN

Written by Sean Callery

Contents

Introduction	2
Early Life	4
Coal Mining	6
Life Saver	8
First Locomotive	10
Steam Power	12
All Aboard!	14
Quick Thinking	16
Victory!	18
Tracks Take Over	20
Steam Railway Timeline	22
Glossary	24

INTRODUCTION

George Stephenson had poor parents who could not read or write, but he taught himself to be an **engineer**.

When George was young, most steam **engines** were used to work machines in factories. There were no cars at that time. Heavy **goods** were sent by canal and people bumped along by cart on dusty roads.

When George grew up, he built light, powerful steam engines that ran on iron rails.

George changed transport forever. He has been called the 'father of **railways**'.

One of George's steam engines

EARLY LIFE

George Stephenson was born in 1781 in Wylam, a village in the north of England. Horses pulled loaded wagons along a wooden track that ran past his house. When he was eight, he got a job opening and closing the gates for them and keeping cows off the track.

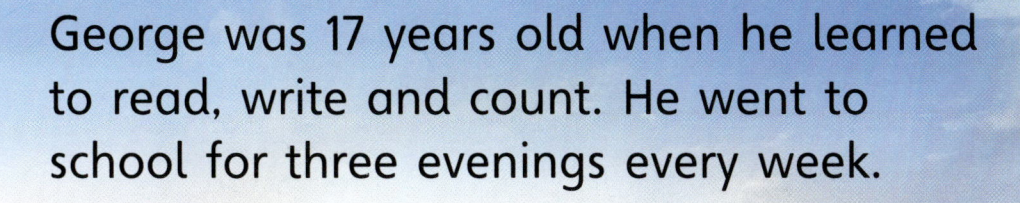

George was 17 years old when he learned to read, write and count. He went to school for three evenings every week.

FACT

George made extra money by making shoes and fixing broken clocks and watches.

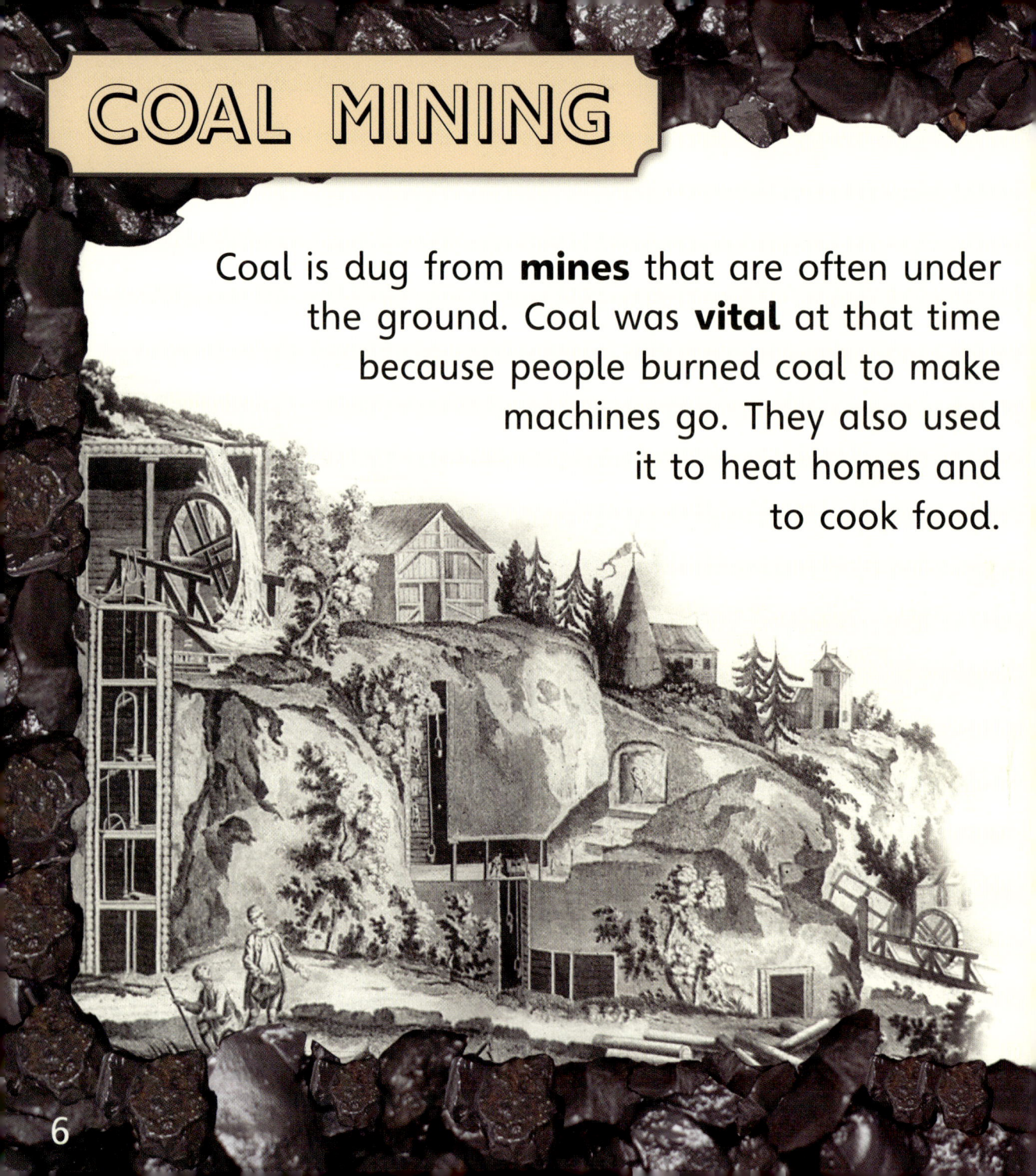

COAL MINING

Coal is dug from **mines** that are often under the ground. Coal was **vital** at that time because people burned coal to make machines go. They also used it to heat homes and to cook food.

George helped his father with his work at a coal mine. They worked the water pumps to keep the mine dry and safe. He saw that the miners used lamps with flames inside so that they could work in the dark.

LIFE SAVER

An underground explosion

In 1812 a huge underground explosion at Felling Pit in the north of England killed 92 miners. Explosions happened when gas from the coal caught alight from the flame in the miners' lamps.

George designed a lamp that used tiny tubes to cut down the flow of air to the flame. So any mine gas that got into the lamp was not enough to explode. The Geordie Lamp saved many miners' lives.

These are all miners' lamps. The one in the middle is the Geordie Lamp.

FIRST LOCOMOTIVE

In 1814 George built his first **locomotive**. It was used to carry loads of coal weighing about 30 tonnes. That's like pulling 30 modern cars. The locomotive rolled on wooden rails at around 6 **kilometres** an hour. That's about as fast as you can run!

George's first locomotive

George's first locomotive broke down a lot. George learned from this and took the machine to bits. He used the parts on some of the 16 locomotives he built during the next five years.

In 1819 George built a 13-kilometre railway line to carry coal wagons. It was the first railway that did not use horses.

FACT People called the locomotives 'iron horses' because they did work once done by horses.

STEAM POWER

2. The burning coal heats the water in the boiler until it boils to make steam.

1. Fuel such as coal is burned in the firebox.

steam

water

FACT

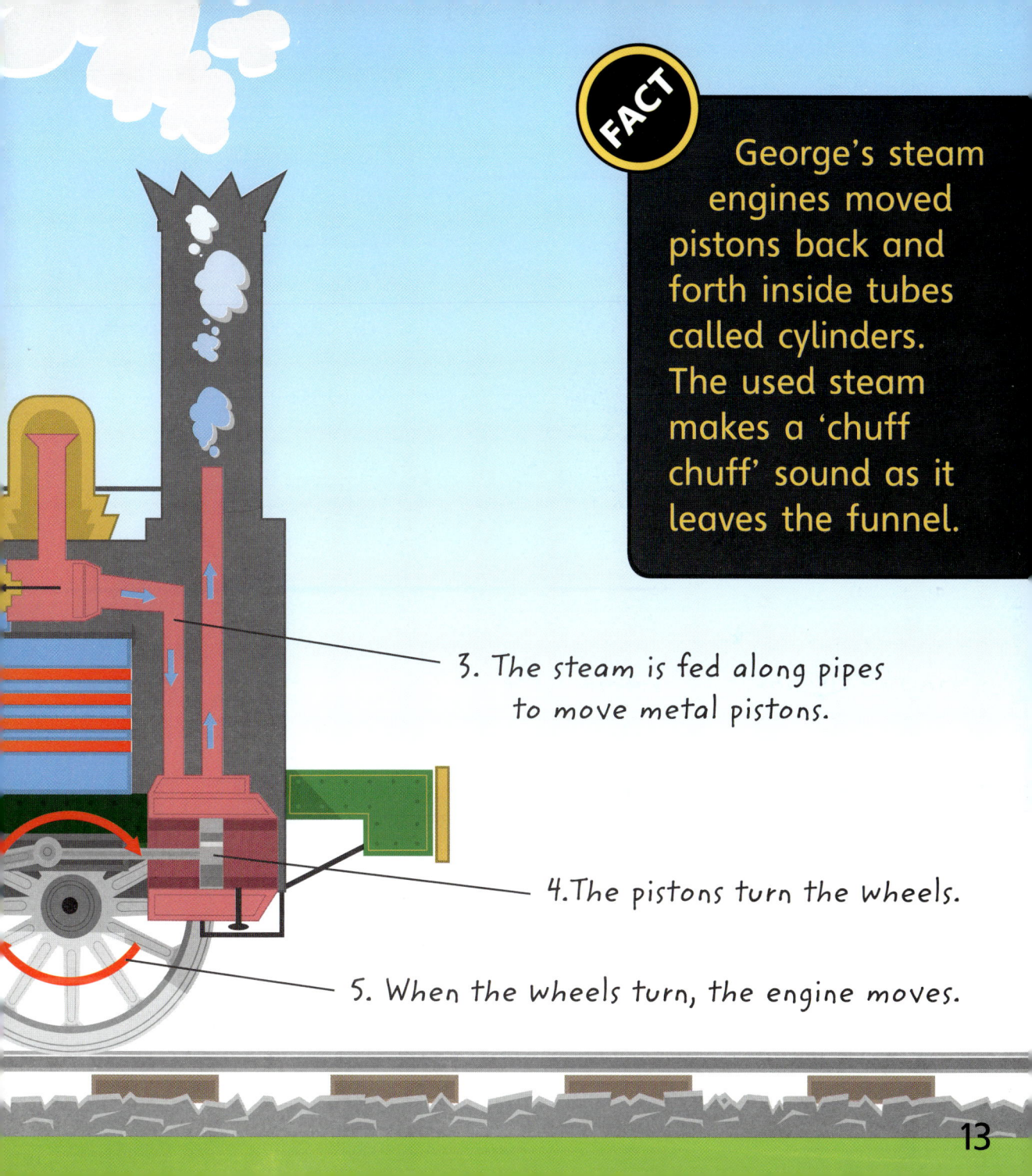

George's steam engines moved pistons back and forth inside tubes called cylinders. The used steam makes a 'chuff chuff' sound as it leaves the funnel.

3. The steam is fed along pipes to move metal pistons.

4. The pistons turn the wheels.

5. When the wheels turn, the engine moves.

ALL ABOARD!

Now George knew how to build locomotives and railway tracks. In 1825 he built the first railway to carry passengers.

It ran 21 km between Stockton and Darlington in the north of England. It pulled 450 passengers at 24 km an hour.

What George learned:

- Locomotives struggled to go up hills and went too fast coming down. So the track had to be as level as possible.

- Longer, stronger rails could be made from a new kind of iron.

← gauge →

FACT The distance between rails is called the gauge. George's gauge is still used around the world.

QUICK THINKING

In 1829 there was a competition to build a locomotive for a new railway from Liverpool to Manchester.

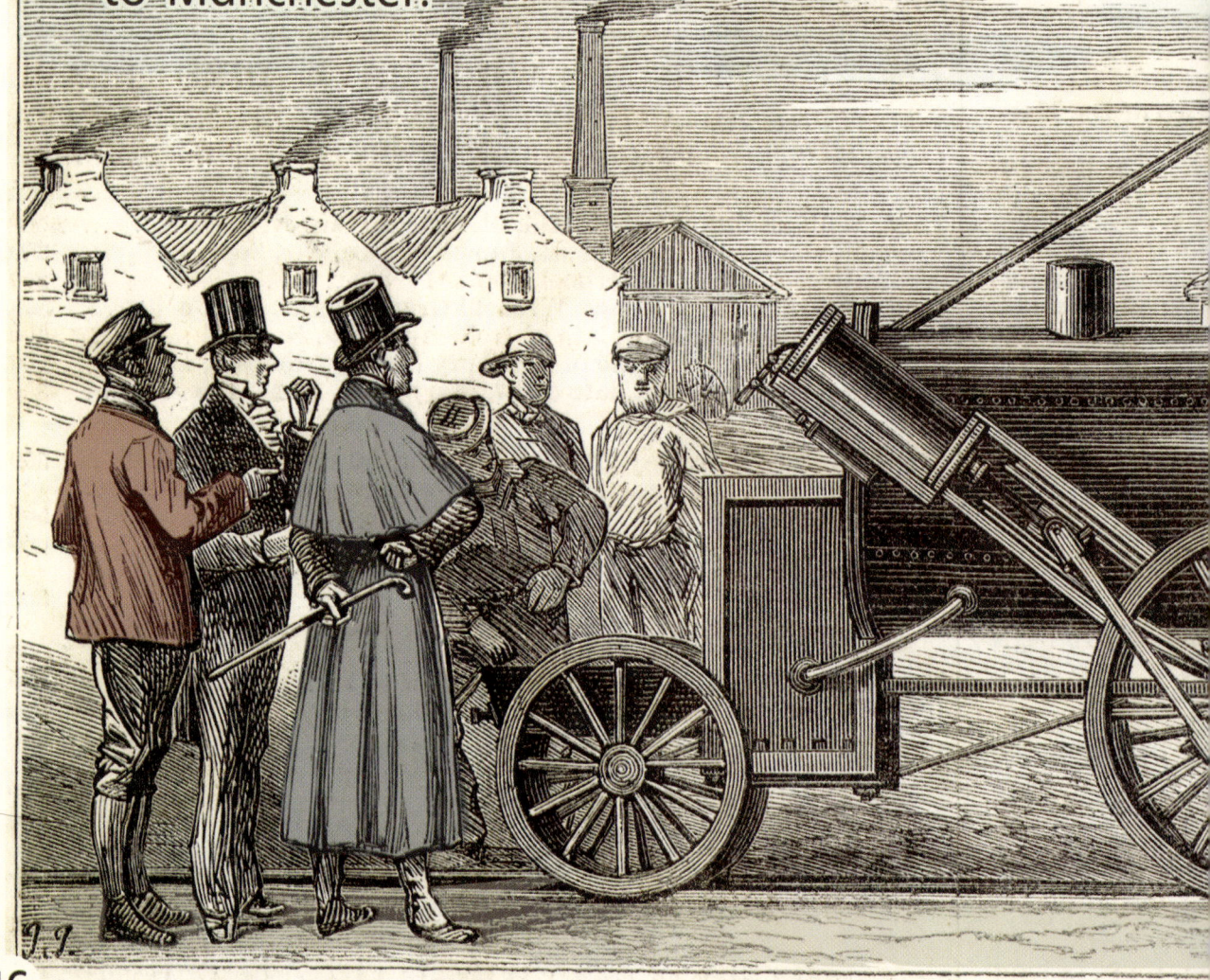

The prize was £500 – that's about **£70,000** in today's money!

The railway needed a very powerful and fast locomotive.

LOCOMOTIVE COMPETITION RULES

- The locomotive must pull three times its own weight.
- It must travel for 48 km at full speed.
- The speed must be at least 16 km an hour.

George entered the competition with his son, Robert. They built a new, fast and light locomotive called *Rocket*.

VICTORY!

Liverpool

31st Octob[er]

ROCKET IS THE

Mercury

WINNER!

Mr George Stephenson and his son Robert won the locomotive competition yesterday.

Their steam locomotive, called *Rocket*, went as fast as 39 km an hour at times.

It travelled 80 km carrying a load of 13 tonnes.

A crowd of 15 000 people cheered when *Rocket* beat the two other trains.

George used a new kind of boiler with lots of heated tubes to make steam more quickly.

TRACKS TAKE OVER

The Liverpool to Manchester railway line was the first long-distance passenger railway service in the world. Nearly half a million people rode on it in its first year.

George carried on building railways until he died in 1848. By then about 8000 km of railway tracks went all over Britain. Many more were built after George's death. Railways began to take over from canals as the best way to carry heavy goods.

FACT George's son Robert was a locomotive builder and bridge designer who became as famous as his father. He worked all over the world building new railways.

STEAM RAILWAY TIMELINE

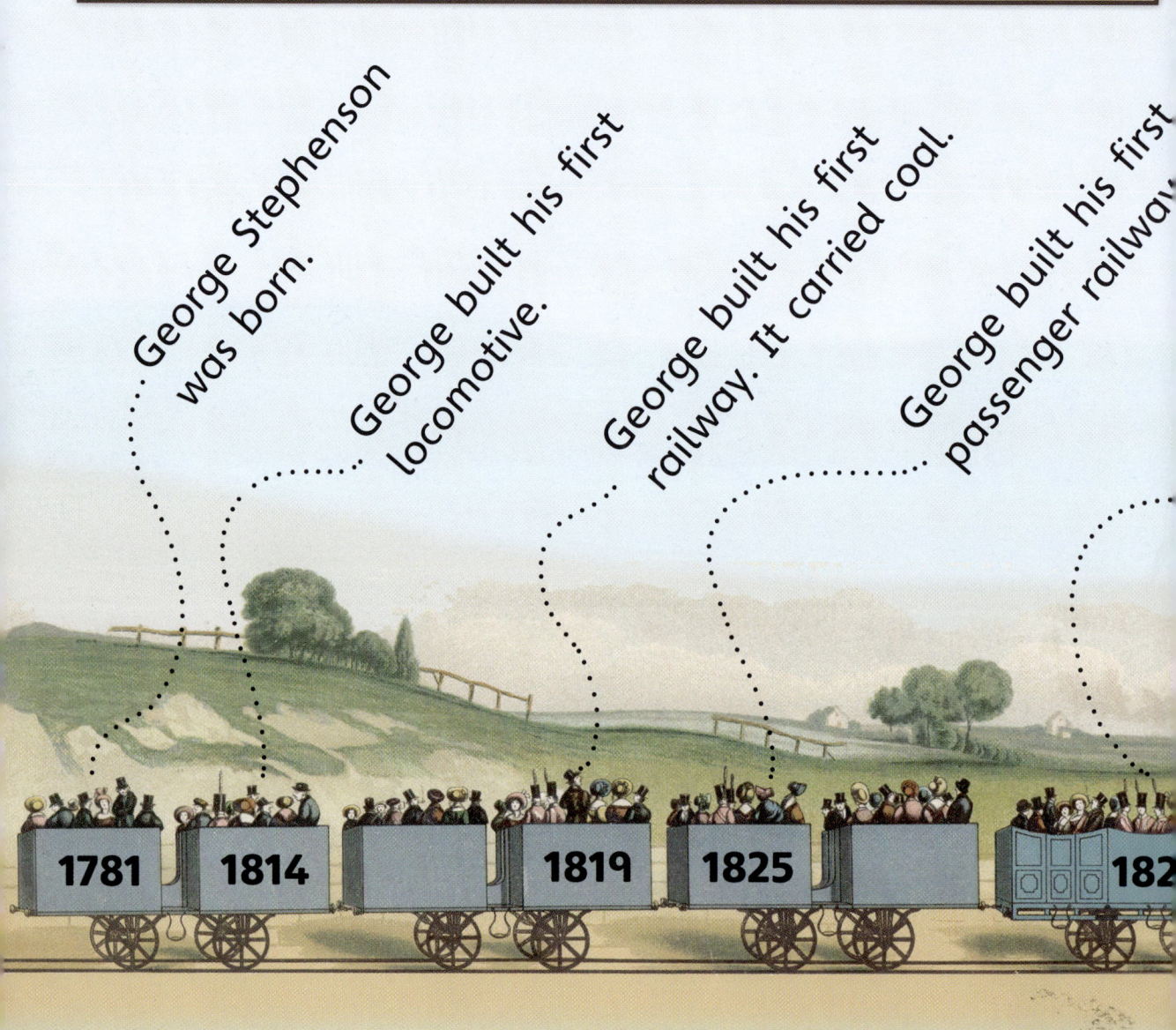

George Stephenson was born. **1781**

George built his first locomotive. **1814**

George built his first railway. It carried coal. **1819**

1825

George built his first passenger railway. **182**

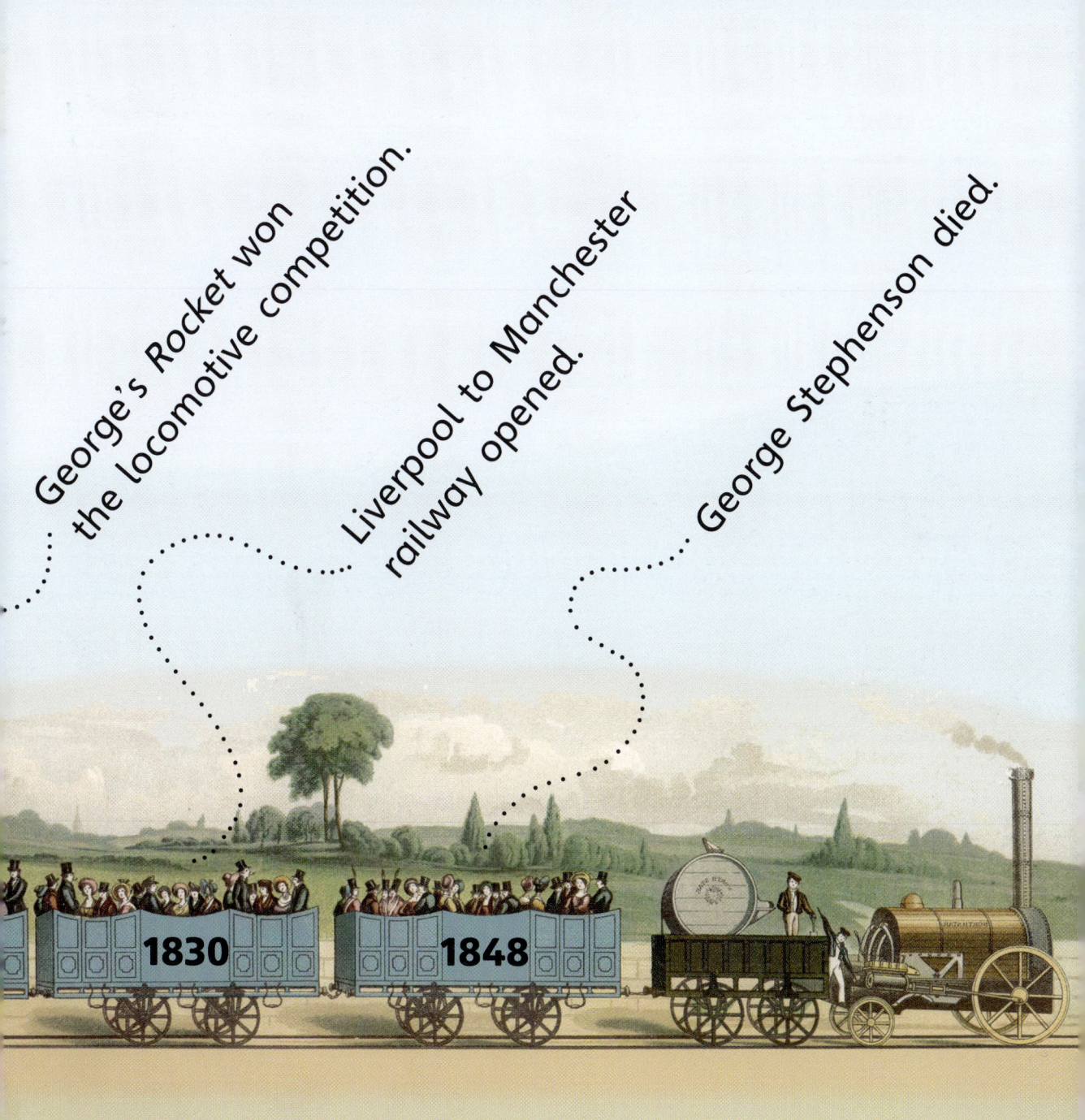

George's Rocket won the locomotive competition.

Liverpool to Manchester railway opened.

George Stephenson died.

1830

1848

GLOSSARY

engine	machine that uses fuel to do work
engineer	someone who makes engines or machines
goods	everyday things that people need
kilometre	one kilometre (km) is 1000 metres
locomotive	moving engine that pushes or pulls railway carriages or trucks
mines	deep holes in the ground from which things such as coal are dug out
railways	systems of railway tracks and trains
vital	very important